AF334893

IN STEREO
Paul Hegedus

BookThug | Toronto *MMVIII*

FIRST EDITION

Produced with the generous assisstance of the Canada Council for the Arts and the Ontario Arts Council.

PRINTED IN CANADA

LIBRARY AND ARCHIVES CANADA CATALOGUING IN PUBLICATION

Hegedus, Paul   In stereo / Paul Hegedus.

Poems. ISBN 978 1 897388 23 5

    I. Title.
PS8615.E32316 2008   C811'.6   C2008-905358-3

for Nicole

[RIGHT CHANNEL 1]

repeat slapstick sequencer limits frequency *repeat run on print formula one step giant leap for mandate* repeat a waxy cylinder scrape by soundscape *repeat container* **repeat** disbelief it or not perforated paper rolls before speakers *repeat speech as first established late nineteenth century reeling* **repeat** oscillation rotation limitation made modification *repeat variable voices* **repeat** visible lines between quadraphonic haiku contortions or tape loop circuitry voice transcriptions to circle swell up slang slug pattern peril response cushion pushing pause *repeat cut out notation* **repeat** a hazard of machine gun trauma *repeat response junkie for more options mr speaker* **repeat** social tranquilizer ray all jerk & no play *repeat slay by play transmission* **repeat** an in line break back beat between typewriter jukebox mood patterns wave for optical turbulence amplification & audio file object generation *repeat a climb the latter screening reordered pages thru flipping function set disordered variation thru slipping* **repeat** scratch invariable turntables *repeat this delay suggests ominous completion plug a comedy of conclusions* **repeat** the present spatial location to generate tabloid soapy solution *repeat hallucination maintain loudspeaker selection election erection stiff joint cover five dollar entrance feedback your projection* **repeat** the drop your work weapons of mass instruction take two steps before bed mate *repeat red state bench press mood display* **repeat** sleaze pass it on *repeat down dynamic noise of generation* **repeat** war head fuckers *repeat use of the letter i the number form circles cough it up sit or set cut line out line no longer than ten minutes* **repeat** to hit rock or page bottom feeder flip out *repeat dead pan bed pan defence pace own face painting pictures naked holes* **repeat** exposure dry your fifteen second wet dream delays expected *repeat a system strewn span disband out banned abandoned out board circular ban saw to in line septic septet gift set a set performance you sonic prize fighter* **repeat** sentence intake conductor less breath less conductive offset valve emergence circuitous wire lacks pauses for breath

the word
acoustic
translates

a word
within this

space

in sights this played

resonant rupture colours voices rising shift
of speech lies elsewhere

a cardboard cut out

time keeping control functions
variable artillery

premature articulation

arcade box animation accumulates
positions at odds are even

surface cushioning for finger
tips performance routine

maintenance quake tip slides as remote
carry on urban splash disguise made decay

cordless fracture stimulant display

increased volume production
suggestion o say

can you see

fluctuations between patterns
questions appearance

early again lifted from five
hours of feature film

what you hear is
not what you heard

then again
before another reclaimed
this not to be expected

turn back & edit the statement in
real time whatever

choice again of artificial flavourings

the corners lifted slightly
five minutes more to release steam

rubberize scavenger
scrub refrigerator rendezvous

suburb prompts
umbrella match

slinking framework sub set

moisten target corners
bullet strike handrail roads
slippery when whet

mumbles fuelled complex episode
within & still

beef brain correspondent
mechanism

rattle click facility

periodic neighbourhood
canopy covering

fabrication or overcoat

to nervous
underdog secretion

haphazard hinges on
forms sonic rotation

headset hindsight

revolutionary waxing
two handed double fisting

design detached in
fingers low weight   aside

subwoofer construction meets
megawatt monologue

monsoon motion tentacle
enterprise

record inscription veers

introduced twice the shaded
single beside a single side

again & flips two shifts

phonographic fizz fare well city

liberties sputter lack lines
running lapse lightly lubricated

private likeness cluster soufflé

rotational knife
tricks circle

pre-amplified greenish
head hits
        a needle in a groove

touch down
twists still

lit white
lights for

fallout funds

        space motto an oboe

headline traps as

strapless statement

headlight striptease

off minor pitch
to slide with ease
a switch a
minute difference

reaction time swings
minimal is condensed
to slow the score

lower (the repeated plays
off genre blur swings a
gain

kit set snared & doing
just fine not

caught without a
flight about time the
leaps the
leaps

the leaps

every day at five another word

tall buildings or single spiral
bound to

speak keeps
hands off

staple activity shaving hairs
for barbershop quintets

playing or
the road less trampled

bullet bound experience
between friends or

what's a different flavour
like old times

an insertion into the ear
produces proven results

discount offer on
bottom of box

superhero submersion
scattering resonant reference

various remains rainy day hit parade

some actions make
for painting
stadium hall patterns

without the kitchen
sink noise machine

regardless of attempts at
acoustics

dimensions not listed as
standard on carton

accents still spinning blues to floor
board action

fabrication wingspan

five minute oppositional cut
off versus

tuxedo disjunction

twist off tactic

seize sea
sick double
edge marathon
run on

footstep to
wheels
thru walls withhold
happening

seeded six string

steady
stayed

pin prick insertion
assertion delusional swells

cherry coke super
store position enhancement

sluggish indoor
nozzle zombie

windpipe forecast discharge

catch grove over take
in step issues plunge

jelly paper jiggle
swept short lights fibre

watch this

finger length to
walls up shoot scars

sometime cellmate
wrecks circus slip
kid cola rental formula

scratch difference plays of wax
over setting a plays compact
champagne

future entrance
knocks ears
to walls up
overlay

sub level striking
blisters yellow suckers

subject enterprise
spiral bondage chambers

branding transparency
conditioner

glow & unglue

scripts stir sonic circles sample solos thru changes voices
uprising hands on split forms a portrait positions plastic
revolutions unheard running mate often masks multiple
photographs torn to twin pieces first fist plunging hinges
on plural replayed high to low oral acrobatics over low
blow aural overdub antics flagging producers of two sided
forgeries & temporary identities logging three legged
traceries or silent sight sketch alias personalities pocket
eyes shape shadow sonic motions measures meaning with
metrics as depth insignificance inches towards surface
suction stone throws free samples but pirates sound
bored off craters or clockwise motion resounding caters
where slip sampling seduction shapes over the counter
top culture strike styrofoam form cut & paste misplaced
rotation shows blue notes shattering radical forces
graphic gestures staggering scribble exchanges hands over
surveillance follows a lexical detector turned nonsensical
defector still functions as fragmentation of symbol &
snare sweating sweet shop sinks to blind finger puppetry
in parliamentary opera buffs shoes in inches towards
surface production encounters covert conversions of
narrative impressions a digression in digestion discharge
carding minors omit major leaps moving thru a spasm
masked splinter or silver sliver sonic slogan for cymbal
suspended borders on false fits where feedback scenario
riddled exhaustion fallen scratches or cardboard clips to
strings scent sentence still staggers this the squeeze play
rhythm of refused clockwork endgame raffle noise caps
surround sounding blisters monotonous misreading for
guttural stress points motions toward seldom staggering
scat shows slang for drag queen monopoly fries & stoke
soprano headlight warfare aggravates the soft serve exterior

[LEFT CHANNEL 1]

curve cries before step

step before curve cries

before step curve cries

cries step before curve

step curve before cries

curve cries step before

q

p

o

h

(

c

(h)ear

delay in without resolution

begins sentence
several times removed

a bin a batch & clean
steps more

yard waste central takes
to positions

loops accept except to pool

eyes closed

counted self several

self serve tied mouth to

mouth to spun underneath

bridge gaps against to

continue a space a

splash retains watched too

sprays with soda send off self

image (imagine a square is a

centre divided substance

throughout

[RIGHT CHANNEL 2]

[popular song material showdown]

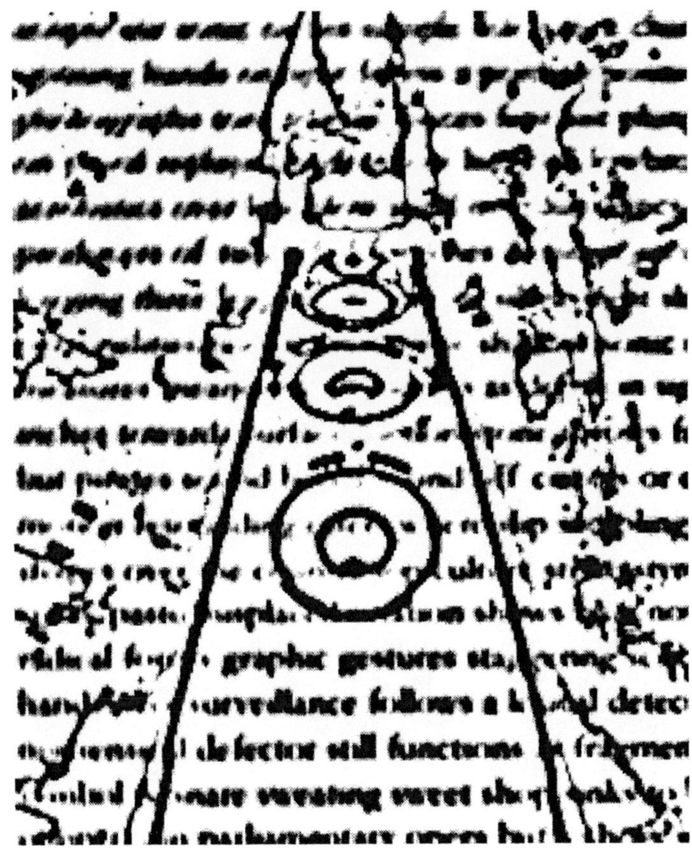

[responsive hand holds a plastic saxophone]

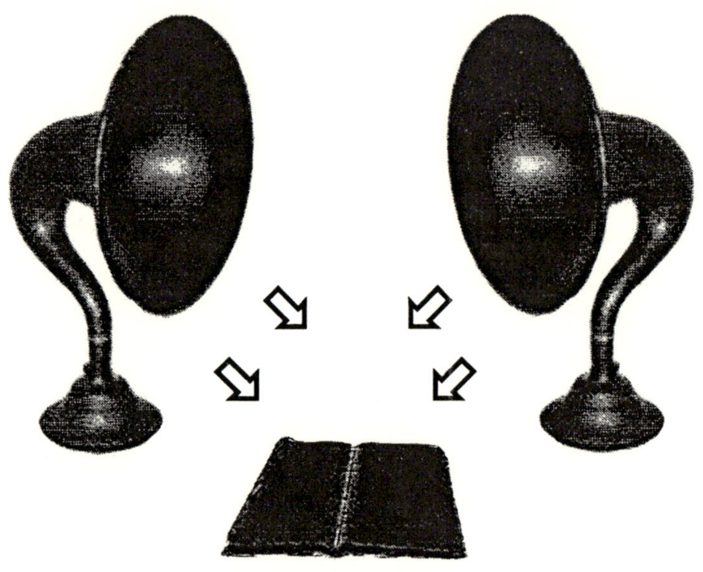

Precise sound picture reproduction relates the recorded
sound field for replay within a second acoustic space.
Accurate playback improves with the proper positioning of
each speaker & an increase in the number of output channels.

In performance, a single speaker transmits in monophony.
Playback by way of two or more speakers increases the
potential for acoustic accuracy in the retransmission of the
recording. Four simultaneous poets speak in quadraphony.

who means how to why or sometimes
why means who to how again to who
means why to where & how means who
or sometimes when

again to who is means to why & why is
how & means to who this leads to how &
how to when & leads this means to what
& who

who to where means how to when or
what to where but how to who though
then when why leads what to when then
what to lead to what to means

[METHOD 7.2 – MANUAL OPERATION]

pinball pipe back paddle ball

scribble in circles then cycle off syllables

subtlety not a forte nor a line
before ballad bawls bowls over

lights flash routine sales checks

work with language but use both
hands or apply water for moisture

operate under cover
some assembly required

run on typography measures
pages to pre-recorded tape

audible illegible

print pint cost this placed meant
initial diction disturbance

the impulse towards theft or constraint

repetition in difference & drops names nobody

scratch junk a dropper next to
revolutions set thirty three & a third

a cymbal twice suspended

attempt elusive details
before allusive splatter

disconnection feedback reference
opposite option operate impulse

invade less graphic match
low life cartoon noise

altissimo speech patterns
rigged resonant residence

orchestral autopilot

lament descending facsimile
the spout set off five degrees

a question paraded over glue

discursive lines up shot put out instant trial offer

fisted frame works fitted bloated body

multiphonic inflection set text
force or implied harmonic

lay out a chorus off the paper
cut five minutes longer to remaster

paper bag playback broke broadcast live again
uncensored

the throw too remote along distance
spin it out of control

| 39 |

this is state of the art equipment

record recovery follow erasure out of time

robber blind buried blanket blonde & baked

out maps later work an edit

rubber labour saving device vending machines

fence set sword over pick it patterns lawn spent plastic
flamingos

glisses glisten icing for corporate card shark cowboys

we call it white collar blue balls

the resolution will not be televised

fill filter an engine illegible muddle at endspace
lacks lie often misguided

housed outside its field haywire & flickt mark
made trivial

a gamble or loose edge placed next to transfer
volume was water movement a repetition

a bucket tosst & at its heights the option as always
cliffs outdoor & content a word angled rain soaked
ink bled thru

surface was sided not once within a margin sees
double

double an understatement & made for under this
lies

freefall motions once the space for errors call it
closed (replay the tape

autosearch again for subtle noises

step in late at times drop early once too harsh the
push plays back

rest rewind read different track the space to switch
in seconds

take turns pages out of earshot

pedal down & echo thru halls

[delay reaction]

border annoys borders a noise

string set certain vibrations the remains movement
straight forward

land open to maintain a place position a marker
the left dot line centre or work from two places
at once

plastic toys sound again mistaken for small car
alarms the bells ring once for room service

two channel stereo sent fly by overnight

silent without included future movement melts
the same returns upon request

speech sets movement towards two words

common binding results in pages facing

clean cuts close to stereo standard

sleeps at eye level once bends nightmares false
alarm

roller coaster drive by

milestones made more frequent flyer drops a
bomb

snare snaps live action caught on tape or rolls the
set in steps right up falls hope

the wheel was once too high shoots lower level
straight the plastic ball let loose

divide draw insert quarter per chance to dream

skin tight races city street in completes the stop

polar opposite attraction sparks dark marks a bourbon
border run on no longer repeating pattern surplus folds
this page into paper cranes or frogs pushed to leap if
pressed tapes surface cling on hand hold sliding head
first basing or basting over boasting afro rose toasting
fine phrases like licks or lines the riff based basis ending
turning on the edit more obvious when dubbing over
double spacing leads to longer lines to first base phrase
layers conversational texture looping pivots trigger
holes bound still to ricochet under stress the line
targets visions of acoustics turned acrostics now set
disorder filled field & throws the dancer off the stage
the hook line & sink or can the canned background
elevator meets escalator edges cluster shapes with fists
the frame remains fried forms where circles strings of
spaces cigarette surface fixture still static motion of a
drone or blank imprint as orchestration fills frames
the wax out fractured factions finding wrong notes
the ideal situation as outlined on page three & still set
salary artillery the breathing marks or scale to require
quiet places over public spaces out paced routine rest
stop pay per view panic assault seats four with fingering
lightly blind libido bozo grease dildo drifts public
access projection system terms the spread or fan based
fan belt dual amplified stereophonic functions as four
part invention meets four on the floor foreplay floors
the lover of intention turned foolproof radio receiver
intervention curbs curtained hauls over hallway
function former of static noise next to night life display
turned delay to that of what without what follows blue
noting surveillance stresses watching out for falling
fixtures famous chambers slide far reaching feed
back behind mix master mikes note necessary noise

[LEFT CHANNEL 2]

She liked to talk and to sing songs and she
liked to change places. Wherever she was she
always liked to change places. Otherwise
there was nothing to do all day.
– Gertrude Stein
Ida

Space is displaced. Question
notion, position
isolation.

Us & them borders over
topples topless tea
pot cozy.

True clothes for comfort. Trades
liquor for lemonade.

Highlight zipper warfare
trench fair less than cotton candy.

Grams over pounds, dollars
& incensed.

Out of time equals out
of order. Whistle shoulders appearance
demo omission.

Unravelling delights.

Stop again. Look out
below. Here the
noise.

Double time shifts overtime.

For the record there were
gaps at the moment of impact.

There's no point like the
present. Thickly coated

as in cakes or pieces of glass.
Adjustments have been made.

Unauthorized copping of this
recording is prohibited.

Some restrictions apply within.
Kicked in & counting.

Cornered coroner. What comes out
in straight lines. Dodging traffic photo replay.

Watch for flashing lights.

Lightning compared to a
lack of lighting.

Lacking or lightening. Lodged to
press shoulders back down.

Footfall substitute. Lost
bandages to block eyeballs.

Mined the gap.

Tunnels wound tight claim to bed
posts springs again
against rainfall.

Slipknot stereophonics.

Clothes herself in scatters clothes
herself in fields herself enclosed.

Flipside switch set upside down.

Instrumentation has been finely
tuned for each operation.

The clicking of flash photography
may produce an echo in certain spaces.

Fingerboard inflection.

Compact recording circuit
faces eight laps & counting.

[

i says what am i says what am i says
what am i says where am i says where
am i says where am i says where am i
says how am i says how am i says how
am i says how am i says when am i
says when am i says when am i says
when am i says why am i says why am
i says why am i says why am i says

                                    ]

Shifts changing guards to blinds
give or take.

Eight hours not ours.

Mirrors used while sixty nining.
                Slides pictures
not pooled

reflections.

Speaker placement as
an element of performance

practice. Sipping club soda
with a sandwich.

Microphones are to
toasting as the

jam is to __________.

Speech set sales record
having hidden hard rod hooks.

Parades posing faces angled interval.
Shipping or wailing trailer for
trumpets.

A pair of feet a float. A
slant. Alias unlimited.

Travelling in twos.

Analog dialogue. Action figure
reaction. Solo sax meets
solo sex. Words scored

or staged for plays the
breaking or sliding of
pitch. The neighbour's grass
like astroturf.

Informs in triplicate.

Decibel levels recorded on
graphs. One sided streets & one

way conversations. Quiet
poets mirror new age musicians.

Last words to the wise guy. Eyes
the pries.

Silver sliver in version.

hearing anticipates

strings amplifier
limit drywall decoder

trapdoor curtain
domino affection

listening recodes

hail to the frozen layer
cooling conquistador

trigger finger abbreviation

overnight discharge recharge
or hands disappearing

the cover of closure.

can be hip to the pothole
loophole

hold
on until

all that remains

exit condition
underscores paint
can gesture steering
mechanism

mood display for traffic
pistol enlargement

time running out of
arms salute listing

skyscraper penetration
leads to over stimulation

a turn for the terse

veering or careening
downtown counts
down towards corners
turning frisbees

high beam lag time
fuelled circular motion

all swell that ends fell

captain america contains typos

savings reports daylight savings

hot dogs in a field of contain
meant going down

smooth move is synchronized in
formation overload

overlord of happy land when
flying pig scratch scaffolding

tables turning tablism

imaginary override next to
surface operation

showroom decompression sets
poetics at volcanics

i've got
two twin cables & a vibraphone

this addition comes unabridged
with line or notes available

note the attention
detail in laid push forward

prop to surplus contrast half
fed letters a rope (a reel

a rise tend off treats five
over sonic gush blue green

layered in layers in another
conversation included
budding building

holding a book
like you carry a tune

finer not so fine
or trades words always on
small pieces of paper

notice the two speakers

your relationship to a
position thru its repetition

split finger mirror figure

flip side rotations of
vocalized versioning

fun house flowers informed
by glass shards

7   Flows and intensities. Perimeter pressing. This is not art for K Mart's sake. Each shimmy massive culture stick shift ultra.

4 I refer to the chief agent zero smoke screen contingent. The static stimulus. Cumulus. Bullet proof of purchase.

10   Structural definitions of linear durations. Highlight solo stamp marks Cineplex Satan. Centralize love songs: meet the late movement freeway.

19 Retro Houdini squeezeplay. Can I get a mango?

[1] Don't buy this. Stolen bases lead to lost causes. Follow line flow line follow.

[8] Retool density value vending material of mirrors. Constraints cause freedoms. Elision exclusion straight schism decision.

[13] Flutter switch material. Never say clever clavier.

[5] Believe me. Developing effective communication is a five step process. Step one straightjacket of the solo sousaphone.

[12] This essay begins with a brief passage of time. Set method of engagement. Never ate, shredded weight.

[3] The majority of these pieces exist. Syntax of the scissors lizard. Editorial dimensions of reading by sight.

[16] Sanity of seismic solo seizing. Traditional sixteenth century performance practice of __________. Accurate maintenance of said practice.

[11] Location on the ever solitary double bill. Lost and found. I'm telling you, there's nothing free about it.

[14] This is music entangles the readiness consumption model stomach of offering. Reading reference citation objection noted.

[2] Hello good buy.

[17] Jigsaw effect of the interior architecture. Pieces in pieces. Follow these simple directions. With strings.

[9] Percussion and precision, precise repercussion.

[18] Notes can be misleading. Ideal. Covered with fixed central rebate of the single social mixdown dear listener.

[20] Frozen fish coating fried forms of fine fur. We can be slaves. I shot the sheriff, but the president is still at large. Never discount the language of transparency.

[6] Jettison. Lament. Rough trade. The existence of God – Scientifically proven! Smother me handling of headphone quarantine.

[15] Scores this reading once sounded out. A circle with a hole in the middle. Repeat as necessary.

lies. timing lies. lacks timing in lies. flat scripts screen
timing it lacks in lies. flat screen lies in. lies flat. flat.
figures flat. paste solo figures flat. figures paste press
& cut a flat solo. cut & paste press. press paste. press.
screen press. in screen press pass. press statements pass
for versions a signal scattering. scattering statements for
versions. statements for. statements. drills statements.
gun statements drills machine. bubble gum machine
gun drills set statements. set gun machine bubble.
bubble gun. bubble. pop bubble. pop radio sonic
bubble. sonic medium refills bubble upsize pop radio
resize. radio medium resize upsize. upsize medium.
medium. fresh medium. often pine medium fresh.
medium pine & lemon fresh often interchangeable
scents. fresh pine often scents. fresh scents. fresh. fresh
for. fresh picket for exchange. fresh exchange walls
for picket fences sense swords. swords sense fences
walls. swords sense. swords. surplus swords. pounding
swords raises surplus. surplus pounding stakes raises
swords a cordless option. surplus option a pounding.
option a. option. drowning option. option a drowning
industry. misery loves industry option a rebate
drowning. industry a rebate option. rebate industry.
industry. swell industry. swell industry rise sensation.
industry spills swell standardization high rise castration
sensation. high spills castration industry. spills high.
spills. static spills. spills stamps static elastic. spills
elastic oddity dotting static stamps symphonic confetti.
oddity dotting symphonic static. static oddity. static.

[LEFT CHANNEL 3]

ACKNOWLEDGEMENTS

Parts of this book first appeared in *BafterC, dANDelion, Existere, The Pissing Ice Anthology, QSQ* and *Rampike.* Thank you to the editors. A portion of this book also first appeared as liner notes for Kyle Brenders' solo saxophone recording *Flows and Intensities.*

Thank you to Kemeny Babineau, Kyle Brenders, Sharon Harris, Jeremy McLeod, Jenny Sampirisi, Dave Worsley and Words Worth Books; thank you to my wife Nicole, and to my parents: Alannah and Tim. Also to Gustave Morin for his piece for the cover of this book.

Thank you especially to Jay MillAr for his support of this project. And to Stephen Cain for his many helpful edits and ideas over beers.

PAUL HEGEDUS is the author of *Noise Present at the Moment Less Clear* (BookThug, 2006). He currently works as a teacher in Brampton, Ontario, where he lives with his wife Nicole.

COLOPHON

Manufactured in an edition of 400 copies in the fall of 2008. Distributed in Canada by the Literary Press Group: WWW.LPG.CA. Distributed in the US by Small Press Distribution: WWW.SPDBOOKS.ORG. Shop online at WWW.BOOKTHUG.CA

Edited for the press by Stephen Cain
Book design by Jay MillAr
Cover by Gustave Morin